Contents

Some words are shown in bold, **like this**. You can find them in the glossary on page 23.

What are the parts of a plant?

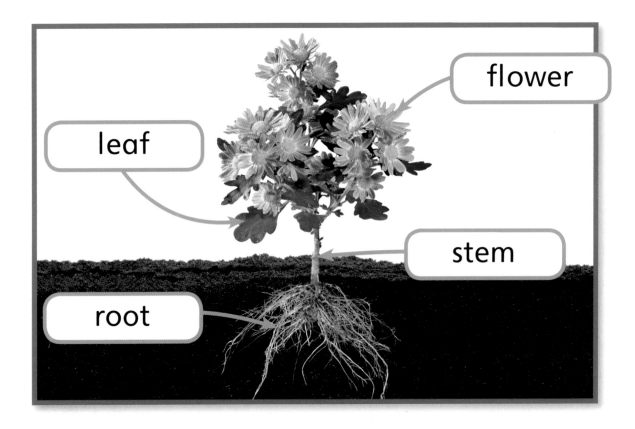

There are many different kinds of plants.

All plants are made up of the same parts.

seeds

Some plant parts grow above the ground in the light.

Most seeds grow inside parts of the plant.

What are seeds?

seeds

seeds

Seeds are part of a plant.

Some seeds grow inside soft **fruits**.

seed

Some seeds grow inside other kinds of fruits.

Nuts are seeds that grow inside hard, dry fruits.

7

Where do seeds grow?

The flowers of a plant make seeds.

The seeds are part of the **fruit** of a plant.

The fruit grows bigger after the flower dies.

There are seeds inside this fruit.

Why do plants have seeds?

When seeds land in soil they make new plants.

The young plants are called **seedlings**.

Seedlings grow into plants.

The seedlings look just like the plant the seeds came from.

How big are seeds?

Seeds come in many sizes.

These poppy seeds are tiny.

Some seeds are very big.

A coconut is a very big seed.

How many seeds can a plant have?

A **fruit** may have just one seed.

An avocado has one big seed inside.

Some plants have lots of seeds.

A strawberry has many tiny seeds on the outside.

Why are seeds different shapes?

seed hooks

The shape of a seed helps it move to a place where it will grow.

Hooks help some seeds hold on to animal fur.

Some seeds are light and fluffy so they blow in the wind.

How do people use seeds?

People use seeds for food.

We crush, squeeze, or pop some fruits to eat the seeds inside.

We can put seeds in the ground.

Later the seeds will grow into
new plants.

How do animals use seeds?

Animals use seeds for food, too.

Birds, squirrels, elephants, and monkeys eat seeds.

Some animals eat the seeds
right away.

Others bury their seeds to eat later.

Count and record

This bar chart compares the number of seeds in different fruits.

Which fruit has the most seeds here?

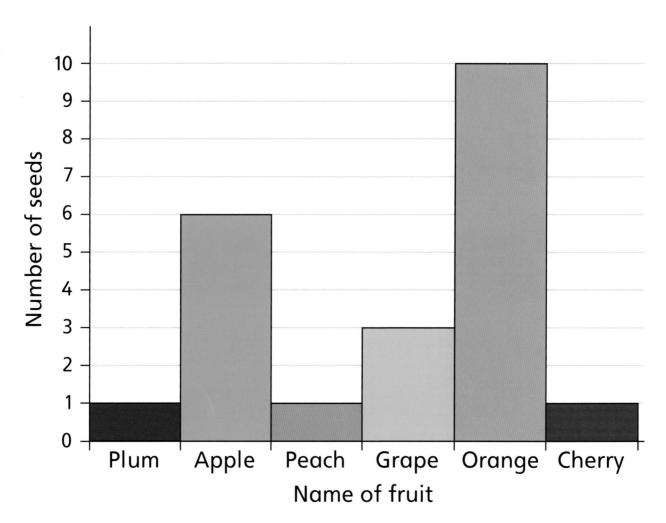

Glossary

 **fruit** the part of a plant where the seeds are

 **hook** the curved part of a seed that catches on to things

 **seedling** the new plant that has just come out of the ground

Index